MW01628698

To My Child... You Are Perfect!

Written by Latimah Clark

Illustrated by Jamel Carroll

This book is
dedicated to
all of the new parents out there
that feel overwhelmed
and need to refuel themselves because
this is hard and I am proud of you!

This book is
also dedicated to
my vibrant, kind, loving, intelligent, and beautiful daughter!
I LOVE YOU SO MUCH!

To My Child...
You Are Perfect Certificate

This is to certify that

____

Weighing _____ lbs. _____Oz. was born

On the _____ day of ___________

to __________________ and ________________

In the year of _________.

From the curls in your hair

to your ten tiny toes,

You Are Perfect!

PU

RE

From your cries of love

to your first words spoken,

You Are Perfect!

INNO

CENT

From the sparkle in your smile

to the joy in your laugh makes it all worth it,

You Are Perfect!

PREC

IOUS

From staring at the beauty in your soul

to anxiously wondering what your future holds,

because...

CUR

OUS

Mommy knows, daddy knows
and the world will know,

YOU ARE PERFECT!

AND...

LOV

VED

Dear New Parent,

If no one has told you, let me be the first to say that you are doing an amazing job! Our role comes with no manual. Even if our role did come with a manual, every child is different, so the instructions would be flawed. Please take it easy on yourself. The both of you are new to each other and are learning together. There is enough pressure coming from everyone else trying to tell you how to raise your child. Do not apply more pressure by feeling like you are failing. Remember, there is no such thing as a perfect parent.

Sincerely,
Author/ An Imperfect Parent

New Parent Recognition Certificate

We hereby Present

You

With this certificate acknowledging

that you are a good parent and are doing a great job!

Latimah Clark

Latimah Clark
Author & An Imperfect New Parent

Latimah Clark is a mother, educator, mentor, career woman and someone who enjoys visual arts.'To My Child...You are Prefect!' is about looking at the imperfect moments of parenthood and seeing them as perfect. This book is inspired by Latimah's experience being a first time mother. Though being a new parent is not easy for Latimah, her desire for her child is stronger than the challenge of parenthood and the many hats that she wears. She is hoping that this book, helps parents remember the purity, innocence, and preciousness of their little one(s).

Pure Innocent Precious Curious Loved
Pure Innocent Precious Curious Loved
Pure Innocent Precious Curious Loved
Pure Innocent Precious Curious Loved
Pure Innocent Precious Curious Loved
Pure Innocent Precious Curious Loved
Pure Innocent Precious Curious Loved
Pure Innocent Precious Curious Loved
Pure Innocent Precious Curious Loved
Pure Innocent Precious Curious Loved
Pure Innocent Precious Curious Loved
Pure Innocent Precious Curious Loved
Pure Innocent Precious Curious Loved
Pure Innocent Precious Curious Loved
Pure Innocent Precious Curious Loved
Pure Innocent Precious Curious Loved
Pure Innocent Precious Curious Loved
Pure Innocent Precious Curious Loved
Pure Innocent Precious Curious Loved

Pure Innocent Precious Curious Loved
Pure Innocent Precious Curious Loved
Pure Innocent Precious Curious Loved
Pure Innocent Precious Curious Loved
Pure Innocent Precious Curious Loved
Pure Innocent Precious Curious Loved
Pure Innocent Precious Curious Loved
Pure Innocent Precious Curious Loved
Pure Innocent Precious Curious Loved
Pure Innocent Precious Curious Loved
Pure Innocent Precious Curious Loved
Pure Innocent Precious Curious Loved
Pure Innocent Precious Curious Loved
Pure Innocent Precious Curious Loved
Pure Innocent Precious Curious Loved
Pure Innocent Precious Curious Loved
Pure Innocent Precious Curious Loved
Pure Innocent Precious Curious Loved
Pure Innocent Precious Curious Loved

Pure Innocent Precious Curious Loved
Pure Innocent Precious Curious Loved
Pure Innocent Precious Curious Loved
Pure Innocent Precious Curious Loved
Pure Innocent Precious Curious Loved
Pure Innocent Precious Curious Loved
Pure Innocent Precious Curious Loved
Pure Innocent Precious Curious Loved
Pure Innocent Precious Curious Loved
Pure Innocent Precious Curious Loved
Pure Innocent Precious Curious Loved
Pure Innocent Precious Curious Loved
Pure Innocent Precious Curious Loved
Pure Innocent Precious Curious Loved
Pure Innocent Precious Curious Loved
Pure Innocent Precious Curious Loved
Pure Innocent Precious Curious Loved
Pure Innocent Precious Curious Loved
Pure Innocent Precious Curious Loved

Made in the USA
Middletown, DE
21 March 2021

36017164R00018